New Issues Poetry & Prose

Editor	Herbert Scott
Associate Editor	David Dodd Lee
Copy Editor	Jonathan Pugh
Readers	Kirsten Hemmy, Erik Lesniewski, Adela Najarro, Margaret von Steinen
Assistants to the Editor	Rebecca Beech, Eric Hansen, Lynnea Page, Derek Pollard, Marianne E. Swierenga
Business Manager	Michele McLaughlin
Fiscal Officer	Marilyn Rowe

New Issues Poetry & Prose
The College of Arts and Sciences
Western Michigan University
Kalamazoo, MI 49008

First Edition, 2003.

ISBN   1930974299 (paperbound)

Library of Congress Cataloging-in-Publication Data:
Sexton, Elaine
Sleuth/Elaine Sexton
Library of Congress Control Number: 2002112919

Art Director	Tricia Hennessy
Designer	Emily Grile
Production Manager	Paul Sizer
	The Design Center, Department of Art
	College of Fine Arts
	Western Michigan University

New Issues Press
269-387-8185
Bound Galleys
www.wmich.edu/newissues

SLEUTH

ELAINE SEXTON

New Issues

WESTERN MICHIGAN UNIVERSITY

in memory of my mother and father

for Robin and Teddy

Contents

Three

Acknowledgments

I wish to thank the editors of the following publications, who published these poems, sometimes in slightly different versions:

The American Poetry Review: "Crime Scene," "Rethinking Regret," "Sleuth"

The Christian Science Monitor: "Family-Style"

Connect: Corpus Issue: "Building a Nest"

5 A.M.: "Code," "Little Boar's Head, on the Map," "Super 8"

Hubbub: "Apostles: Black & White"

The Marlboro Review: "The Flag of My Disposition"

Mars Hill Review: "Contrition"

New Letters: "Neighbors," "Public Transportation"

Prairie Schooner: "A Tongue on the Road," "The Crack in a Word," "Hair Treatment," "Savings," "Totem"

Rattapallax: "Hotel Recamier," "Subterraine," "Nora, a Novel"

Rivendell: "Summer Vernacular"

River Styx: "Nuclear Fruit," "The Pitch Forward"

The Women's Review of Books: "Winter Climate," "Undressed in The Cloisters"

You Are Here: The Journal of Creative Geography: "The World Book"

My thanks to the editors who published the following poems online: "The Trade of Escape" (in *Frigate*), and "Coming & Going" (in *On The Page*).

"Undressed in The Cloisters" scored the text and movement for "Mix," a dance by Daniel McCusker performed at Tufts University, December 1999.

In addition to those mentioned in the dedications, I'd like to thank John Kramer, Daniel McCusker and Tom Mohan for their friendship and feedback. I'm grateful to all the writers who gather at 7 Carmine, in particular: Curtis Bauer, Martin Mitchell and Jeet Thayil, for their careful reading of this manuscript in its various stages.

One

Crime Scene

Nothing actual happened in the schoolhouse
girls' room on the island. It just looked like
something could. The scrubbed green & black
linoleum floors stretched under tubs and toilets
made of porcelain and closed up in oak stalls.
A mop & bucket in the corner might have been used
to disturb evidence. By mid-morning a weak light
pressed through the Coke-glass windows
set near the ceiling. "Made in America"
stained the bottom of spotless white basins
I examined in my hour of exile from lessons.
This is where I know the Sisters of Mercy
bathed naked on their summer retreats,
and later sent their failures—like me—to think
about sin. Without instruction. I sat on the rim
of a white tub and tried to make the connection
between evil and not remembering how to spell.
I gave up and resolved to be like Houdini,
to practice the trade of escape. This I would
learn to do with finesse. To be present, but gone.
The refinement came later. But now,
when the hall bell rang, my episode ended.
Recess brought dozens of girls, dressed like me,
swarming in. I flung my cell door open
and joined the flood of others in a rush
of pushing and flushing. I was spinning
in place, not knowing, exactly, what to do.
When no one was watching I forgot, and forgot,
and the forgetting, eventually, became me.

Over My Head

I mean *literally* upstairs on the 9th floor
they make things, manufacture caskets
I imagine, ghoulishly sorting out sketches
at their desks. The long rolling bolts
cross floorboards all day, stockpiled
body containers. After hours,
Korean workers join me and Latino
young men from the mailroom in the cage
of the service elevator. The Irish operator
draws the lever that locks us
together. We descend past the backsides
of business, discarded layouts, trashed
prototypes, coated wires and waste
plastic dumped from the 5th floor
Uniform & Supply, from the 4th floor
Human Hair Wigs, and the new tenants
on the ground floor, the toy business in town
for the fair, once a year, the grown-up men
dressed as action figures, their doughy creations
made for kids, nothing so distant from life
as the Mylar-pink masks in their plate-glass display.

The Lid of Her Life

Her body is an empty address,
the journey's gone out of it.
Against tradition, I choose
not to look at the body.
I pace the park outside
and wait for someone
to close the lid.
That is not my mother in there,
I murmur to the stone monument,
the war dead of Portsmouth,
State Street, icy with snow,
melted, then frozen over.
I'll break my neck in these heels
I've put on to please her, the pearls,
her mink coat, right out of storage.

Undressed in The Cloisters

I am showing you everything as it occurs
to me, so it comes out unfinished,
the truth, before the hoop skirt of fiction
covers its long legs, concealing its shape.

I have ditched the corset and dispensed
with the slip. Everything embroidered is
gone. I, who love tapestry, reach for
bare walls—let the story, allegory, go.

I traded my garments—mazed gardens,
pale virgins, a leaping gazelle—for the
light limbs of language, unclothed
authentic threads, their erratic loose ends.

12

Contrition

This morning I woke with my old prayers intact,
penance in my head. Mary, full of grace.
I'd forgotten these lines, years ago. And I lay still,
alarmed to recall them. What has stuck over time
is the pulse of the words like a poem
learned by rote. When the words fled,
their shape stayed like a womb, full of grace.

I sound them out now, my face pressed on cotton.
I watch a brick wall, from my bed, ruddy
with light, there where the window cracks open,
the arms of dark elms sprawl, empty, against it.

Winter on Earth,
as it is in Heaven.

A Tongue on the Road

Here's the part of the Mass I hate, where
you have to say to strangers, in words

you'd never use in life, "Peace be
with you." When you do this you have to

embrace bodies in a way that's not natural,
not even at a party with cocktails. We are

bundled in coats. It is winter. The church
is stone. All through the gospel a young woman

two pews in front rubs her son's back,
then his head, his shoulders. She is tugging,

and tugs him closer and closer, tighter than
even he, clinging back, wants to be.

She searches his whole body to soothe him.
Or herself. I wish she would stop.

My mother is crying. I draw her temple
to my lips. She is mourning a loss, her

husband. She wants me to take Communion.
I won't. It's enough I'm here at all.

I look back to see who's in the balcony,
singing. I remember the toll booth attendant

last night on my long drive home
and imagine she says, "Go in peace,"

though mine is a journey she only takes fares for.
She is a god or a saint she doesn't know

she invokes. She trails, as all strangers do
in a dream. A tongue on a road,

empty, a speed dangerous
and high. She is a summons,

a siren. A chill in the night. Air.
A handout. An idea.

She is what it takes
to get there.

Hotel Recamier

Ten years later I could swear
the old orange spreads are now
curtains. We traded our double in back
for more light and this view. The narrow
single beds are brand-new and we
push them together, a familiar gesture,
the first night. The chambermaids
are used to this. They smooth out the sheets
every day, our way, spreading the blankets
sideways to cover the crack. I am at ease
with this, this time, but find it hard
to be here with someone else.
I did not plan on this very room,
the same cast-iron gate on the terrace,
the toilet, bidet, the same coarse towels,
faulty faucet. The water in Paris scalds me again,
this time for bringing you.

What Comes Back

It's a new pleasure born
in a small bag of carrots,

chiseled, and a pocket of pita,
split and stuffed with something

new each day. Your hand,
let's say, in my mouth.

The packing
put it there,

when I saw how you
used the reusable pouch

from the bread to hold
this moment in.

And here's the best part:
this tiny plastic thing?

The piece that holds
other bags shut,

that carries the price,
and the date freshness expires?

You used this, too,
for the fruit.

What left the tree
just a few days ago,

gold & a misshapen red,
and not shiny with wax

but dull with the warmth
that picked it. Not since

those old hard days
of money trouble,

growing up where
nothing was tossed,

everything was used:
rubber bands from the iceberg,

string & screws
stuffed in the drawer,

any blank piece of paper
for scrap, jelly jars,

and perfectly good
bruised fruit.

Things were made to be used
& reused. Not since then,

that truth, have I felt a pear
in my palm like this.

Lunch Hour

Harold and I were heartbroken when the old optical shop
closed and the rotating door with bronze pulls stopped
turning. We sat on a park bench in the shade of the Flatiron
by the empty corner store and box-shaped high-rise
built next to it. When *Restoration Hardware* opened for business,
the shopping bags divided and new things made to look old
dropped in: rose-colored tumblers, stainless Martini picks,
pince-nez with black ribbons, an hourglass no one will ever use.
Harold buys his Haitian cigars across the street, where painted
wood Indians, Native Americans, stand on display.
Today, the pretty blonde who serves him, a flirtation he savors,
shows us a picture of her live-in girlfriend, a dark beauty
she keeps in her hip pocket, under plastic, in a century-old
wallet, hand-stitched, a gift her grandfather gave her.

The World Book

Here's the idea, silkworms spinning in the shade of paper parasols,
on dusty streets in home movies, where my sisters actually have to dip
under blossoms to see. And steel shadows, their dark rungs, glide by me
me swaddled in pink cloth rising *blip blip blip*
up the cinematic center of a skyscraper in the City of Lights,
and elsewhere waves crash under our windows,
and the tower is bent, and there's row after row of scent.
We're in so many places, an encyclopedia might be tempted
to look *us* up. Kyoto, Fort Knox, Pittsburgh, Pisa, Rye Beach,
Melrose, Amsterdam, Paris, Verdun, Ipswich, Fort Devens
and more. Could I get more *specific?* There,
where my father died, where they met, where my brother,
John, was born, where I was born, where *they* lived, where *we* lived,
where we *almost* lived, where he, my father, was born,
where my mother was small, where for me, and for good,
    the whole world
opened up. There, where my mother went door-to-door,
but not too often. When she had to, she stopped. After all her friends
& neighbors bought. Where she tried to sell *The World Book*
to those she'd never met, who'd never seen what she had
seen, where Joan of Arc was burnt at the stake, where pilgrims
left their crutches, where soldiers raped the virgins of war,
found giant conch shells to take home, where the kings of France
were crowned, that cathedral, my baptismal site,
where blessed water was dripped
over my head. And years, not too many years, later
the hands that held me over that Gothic font
and lifted me past its iron grates
knocked on the blank doors of strangers in Rye Beach.
And only now, today, when we look up "ginkgo"
to see how that old herb might restore her memory
in this blue bound *World Book*, under the letter "G," she says to me
so I see her feet at the threshold where she stands and her eyes stay,

Elaine, she says, looking back, maybe, for the first time, as if
thirty years were enough to lift any ordinary shade,
those doors were so big.

The Crack in a Word

That day I learned a new word.
It slipped from her mouth with a slap.
"Never *contradict* your mother," she said,
making her self the third person
in a story I'd never forget. I tried
to curb her words with the truth,
in the kitchen. I tugged at her blouse
to stop her from telling the neighbor
what I thought I knew best.
I had never been hit. Not once.
Not since. It was swift.
Her hand flew from her apron
and struck my face. Smart.
Each syllable broke like a post
in a fence, at a border where
the head smolders while the heart
learns to love reason, where it splits.

The Flag of My Disposition

The free end of the flag snags in a beak
at the top of the pole. It tears and tears,
caught in a gust. The stripes strain, the threads
shred with each angry twist. This sail snaps
to nowhere. A mean wind takes me there.
Where everything stalls. Even a blow
gets marooned, and stars won't move.
They stare and stare from where they're fixed.
Right there, where the same groove gets deeper
and deeper. Hear that clink of the rope?
It's not a way out. But the same thin way in.

Thanksgiving

My mother, the harvest moon, the beach at night,
join my brothers, our neighbors, a bonfire,
the jeep we ride in to get there. My niece
rests on my knees. This army blanket appears
in home-movie footage, reels and reels
of gatherings, of surf pounding in them, silent
as dreams. My sisters' arms move to make motion
on screen. The Super 8 colors fade over ocean.
We set the table with you—memory. The knife,
the fork, the main course we consume—is you.

Sewing, a Sonnet

Tonight I squint to thread a needle.
I hold it in my hand, an arm's length

away from the body, to see, and see
the space I once entered helping

my mother, my small fingers reaching
for hers an arm's length away

from her body, her eyes squinting,
my own sharp and ready to help.

Her free arm held me on her lap.
I wedged myself between her

and her unnamed unhappiness,
and pulled the white cotton

thread through an opening so small
only a child could see through it.

Sleuth

I become type on the page, Nancy Drew,
girl detective, solving mysteries

in a series of plots from the tower of books
by my bed. Downstairs the bookcase

my father built, too packed to hold mine,
holds his: *Mein Kampf* in German,

Greek classics, Russian grammar,
an atlas bound in leather,

the entire *World Book*. My father is dead.
I know him by what he collected

and read. He lives in Kodachrome film,
home movies, in his cufflinks, fountain pens,

in the stuffed sea turtle that swims in dust
in the basement. I learn nightly the secrets

of reading. The code. *The Clue in the Crumbling Wall*,
The Witch Tree Symbol. I play the part of Nancy

in the woods by our house, reenact *The Quest
of the Missing Map*, find sense in a tree's bark,

in letters my father wrote my mother,
in what she wrote back, wartime lovers.

Had my father lived, he might have sought my advice
the way Nancy's seeks hers, confiding his conflicts

in private, in his den. I prop my chin on the page,
follow the mystery of a father in fiction,

guiding his daughter, of my father guiding my mother,
in love. Nancy is forever missing a mother;

I cling to mine. I learn how my mother cuts patterns
for dresses in the kitchen, how she lands planes

from a tower as a WAC. My father is forever
missing. I puzzle over how this comes together

in print. I uncover new words, a girl named *George*,
villains in *bungalows*. Nancy rushes to the crime

scene in her yellow *roadster* in my head.
I dismantle my father's wireless recorder

on the porch, his voice too rusty to catch when
liquid mercury breaks from a glass tube inside,

and folds, cold, in my palm. I let it bead on Formica.
Nancy needs no one. I like this idea. Her father

needs *her!* She is fearless and calm. She makes
men tremble. I torment my brother, who grabs

at this magic I play with. We're stunned to see
mercury sucked from his hand, swallowed

whole in the pores of his ring, my father's.
The Mystery of Alchemy in reverse, the gold band

turns silver and mute. Nancy finds a home
for an orphan, an heiress, her fortune.

I discover the cost of curiosity;
I have the tools for detection.

Nancy has what she needs, she's forever eighteen.
The Mystery of the Tolling Bell unfolds.

I don't know till the last page, the last line—
whom to trust. Each day I betray the secrets

of the white clapboard house where we lived,
the mystery of the missing keys to our untuned piano,

the reason a life-size statue of the Virgin Mary
sways in the trunk of the car, today,

as we drive to the dump. Memory is murky.
I follow the clues, the words, the quest for the dead,

for the father, the daughter always led by the author,
the flashlight as it moves in her head.

Totem

She once stood up between pines, a symbol
of faith I didn't buy—the Virgin Mary,

her stone toes buried in tiger lilies.
She rests now in the trunk of my car

on the way to the dump. Her placid gaze,
her image always an embarrassment,

a joke, a landmark for finding our house.
Her body a monument caught in headlights at night

as my dates turned their cars in our drive.
One summer Aunt Dorothy from Pittsburgh

painted Mary's flesh pink, her robes blue,
and my job was to wash her back

to white. The Virgin came with the house
bought from another aunt: Ruth, the ex-nun.

The day we climbed out of the Rambler
into our new yard, my brothers found

the chicken coop, my sisters the basement.
I hung on the statue, picked pine cones

at her feet. We ran from the house
down the road to the beach.

This was our new life without a father.
We learned how to keep my mother

in our hip pockets, wrap her tight
around our little fingers. We stopped kneeling

by our beds to pray before sleep and indulged
in our fears, our imaginations. We heard

the hazards of riptides, how an orphan
from Boston drowned under our aunt's care,

how the Mother of God was placed in the yard
to make amends. *How could it?* I'd ask her,

mouthing the words to deaf ears, her carved veil
unmoving. Every day I crossed her path to post

the mail, sand and salt from the beach
stuck to my legs. The summer I was ten

she was exactly my size. Some days I'd balance
my feet on her base, wrap my body around hers,

taste plaster splintered down her spine.
I'd whisper: *Where's my father?* or

Find my mother a new husband.
I knew it was voodoo, even then.

Two

Summer Vernacular

Rolling pin and meat grinder, wax paper wrap, Salada Iced Tea, the torn skin on a lilac tree branch, Lourdes water in a jar, Sea Road, Hunter's Lane, Aunt Mardie's cottage out back, the hook & eye lock on the door to the bath, burnt orange pine needles, holes in screened windows, scapulas, sachets, pancake make-up, charm bracelets, surfboards, beach sand on the kitchen floor, the Mother of God in the front yard, the prickly bushes with thorns on the path, bare feet, the back steps, the milkman, the mailman, a black Mercury Comet and pink Sting Ray bike in the drive, the neighbor boy in the shed, the Big Scoop, the waves, swimming in rainstorms, riptides, sleep-overs, ice-blue bug zappers, sunburns, mosquito-spider-bee bites, salty skin, wet towels, frizzy hair, letters, mold in the books, dusty drawers, army blankets, Dad: "deceased" on a card, mother's thimbles, Hummels, talk radio, Singer sewing machine, St. Jude's Thrift Shop bargains, the Enhance Your Vocabulary One-Word-A-Day lessons, *The World Book,* the neighbor's twins, Keenie, their old German shepherd put down, lawn mowing, crabapples, hornets' nests, the dirt tread cut through grass under the rope swing.

Neighbors

Old Mrs. Trefetheren lived alone next door
in the apartment over the barn.
I was the one who carried her gifts,
Tollhouse brownies, white lilacs
in season. I saw how she watched our house
through eyebrow windows, the yard smothered
in snow, crabapple blossoms in June.
Avon's Skin-So-Soft and scented talc
wrapped in foil at Christmas. She viewed
our comings and goings, the perilous drops at night,
sneaking out to the half-roof below. I brought her pears
from our tree. And she had to see my brothers and sisters,
the five of us, scaling the shingles and sills, slamming
and shutting doors, locked and leaned on in the dark,
the necking in cars, the sitting on steps,
the washing of sand from our feet coming in
from the beach, the clothesline stripped,
then filled, the changing of storm and screen windows,
prom gowns, sun suits, the mowed and unmowed
grass, the leaving for school, church, graduations,
the coming back from camp and college, the moving out
and moving in from new homes and apartments,
the horns honking, the name-calling, the dinner bell,
the gathering, the divorcing, the dividing.

The Prickly Bush

She protected us by keeping us, by not letting my aunts
take us when my father died. Defenseless, she needed us
like our house needed the green hedge, its prickly thorns
needing the hard red berries we'd get at to taste
their yellow insides. She pulled us in close,
like a cloak, to keep the pain out. She was full of fear
and without strength to protect us from the outside.
And we clung to her like religion, like loose things,
magnets in a metal field. We were her shield, yet we
had none ourselves. We became sharp, quiet, defensive.

Ice Fishing

Once, home from school, I fished Eel Pond at night,
the only girl to skate with the boys who lit small fires
and chopped holes in the ice. Wood splints fit crosswise
in the spaces, and red flags were set to flip up when a pike
caught the line. I wore my mother's coat, boiled wool,
long-waisted, bell-shaped. The blades on my skates flashed
by the fire. Everyone else had a flask. I did not fear
falling in. I had done that before. I accepted their rum.
We rested on snowbanks and waited, and later watched
live fish heave and go still. Pond water spilled from the edge
of their flesh. Northern pike, they lay silent on the surface
with one gold eye open, and only the stars to look up to.

The Splinter

In 1962, Aunt Edith's place in town overlooked
the fifth-floor apartment of her friend Edna Dish.
In Boston that spring, my brother and I slid
in stocking feet down her long oak hall while
my mother went to Mass. The fire escape girdled
windows on two walls, barring our view. Cracked
pots of begonias and geraniums hid us
from Edna, who thought she and my aunt were alone
when she crooned from her kitchen—*darling*—between
buildings. She was courting the aunt my sisters
called spinster. Angry Aunt Edith! whose arms
went limp, listening. We colored books on the couch
as she watered the plants parched over our heads.
That whisper! My mother rang the bell. We raced
to get there first. I slipped on wax and caught
a thick splinter in my foot. City wood.

Enclosures

I dig for replacements in her button box.
Sometimes a bit of fabric clings

to the metal backing of a clasp,
a perfect match hangs by a thread.

I hold the past lives of apparel, a snap,
an embroidered enclosure

in my head. I retrieve every part
of a torn blouse, a worn vest

she stripped for parts, pearls
snipped from a bodice, bone knobs

cut from their beds. An old zipper
lines the back of a new dress.

Lace and elastic seek re-employment.
I run my palm over jagged teeth,

unmatched seams of a striped shirt.
I dust my mother's shiny black Singer,

her foot on the pedal, the hum she'd
retreat to, the needle and bobbin.

Nora, a Novel

She was named for her father's mistress,
Nora. And my father restored her
to Eleanor. He coaxed her to leave
the common, and erase all that slatternly love.
I draw a line from there to here. A string
of the unsaid. The hurt that is truth
becomes fiction. Her father remains
ungrieved, as though the dead owed
nothing to the living. We have nothing
to savor but this: what is said out of breath,
out of time, out of a simple thing, a stringed
instrument, a banjo described.
How her father played it when he taught
her to dance, the place in the corner
where it stayed when he left
and their house became quiet,
a haven where her mother found peace
and my mother learned the secret of leaving,
found peace in my father's pluck, who drew
the best chords out of her, the ones
she learned to play for herself.
The not going back, the never giving up,
and never letting go of the private,
the parts that are sung in the soul.

Code

He was dining at sea with friends
when it happened. His invention.
The telegraph. Samuel Morse. The Morse Code. He was manic,
depressive, an artist. He was frantic, rigid, impolitic.
He ran for mayor and lost. He hated Jews and Irish.
He found abolitionists demented.
He made gardens. And would not quit
until Congress approved. His method. It changed
everything. Made him famous. He painted
and hated portraits. He lectured
and married his cousin. He sued. And won,
and was rich. The code is retired, now. A satellite
relays distress signals that once defined
distress. The sound
and light. The language.

Little Boar's Head, on the Map

cuts into the coast, a snout of stone
licks the sea back each time it is hit.
This is how a shape gets its name.
The point in the road turns
angry, just a little mad,
so your hairs bristle a bit
at the bite the Atlantic is taking.
Time takes shape for granted.
I wait for the swoop the car
makes with us in descent,
what we call a hairpin
in romance or detective fiction.

Pavilion

Remember the storm last summer
on the stone coast of New Hampshire
that ruined the wedding party,
made up of roses, plucked and placed
every few inches on lattice that covered
the chuppah, an Old World custom,
that day on the great green slope
of the New World? The groom's people
and the bride's were lifted off chairs
on the lawn, their linen and tulle,
lace and starched cotton flew and flapped
with the satin in a tornado wind that bit
at the sky, quelling the celebration;
and the rabbi stayed trapped in debris
on the turnpike, and the golden retrievers
and lap dogs strayed from their owners,
the priest was afraid, and left. The children
were thrilled with the storm, their parents
happy no one was hurt, and the couple,
who escaped the collapsed pavilion,
were married later, by a clerk, as the pink sorbet
melted, and the rabbits ate arborvitae
and spilled vegetables, little baby carrots
that dotted the grass.

Happy Birthday, Mom

Let's not forgive the sister forgetting
the reason to celebrate, let's not let
the mother off the hook for having
a stroke, let's not understand anything
unexplained, the time spent, the memento
thrown away, the missed chance to say
something soft when a cushion is needed.
Let's not be kind, let's not hope
for the best. Everyone is busy, everyone
has a life, lessons, openings, races,
a better place to be. Let's not get together,
and say we did.

Hair Treatment

I am looking at you.

And Nora is fixing my hair,
a home-beauty treatment.

You are looking at us.
We are already the past

when the flash goes off.
A fiction begins with you

imagining what you see
and how this story ends,

the evening, the blow-dry,
the combing, the fingers,

the eye shaping the way
we look in another light.

Super 8

We are waving, swimming,
waving, the salty mounds break
over our heads. We are waving,

kicking, swimming, the sea grass
sticks to our legs. We are leaving,
waving, drying our faces on towels

pulled from the line. Wet hair sticks
to our skin like sea grass, the salt
dries like snow on a shell.

Family-Style

When my sisters worked nights at *Yoken's*
Sea Food Restaurant, once each summer
my mother took my brothers and me out to eat.
We leaned from the Rambler's four windows;
everything green rushed in. The wind seemed to suck
color from leaves as they raced along with us, driving
in from the beach. "Thar She Blows" in quotes in neon
blazed in the spout of a whale festooned over the lot.
We were hushed by white linen on tables, the wait staff,
and art on the walls, the "Moby Dick Contest" in full swing.
My sister's entry hung large in the lobby, a dramatic
harpoon poised over the maitre d'. The summer
my brother climbed to top scorer for Rye
Little League, I danced my solo in Tchaikovsky's
Swan Lake. We stood under a swathe of oils on canvas.
Ruddy lobsters clung to platters over our heads.
We were a family, the stars of our own feature film—
we were the artists, the patrons, the summer help.

Encryption

This is an elegy for the stuffed sea turtle
who swims in dust on a shelf in the basement.
This is a hymn for the cracked teacup's myrtle
vines in Rosenthal china. This is a requiem

for the scrapbooks, the dog tags,
a wedding band's run-down rosettes,
the Stars & Stripes, the folded flag;
my mother's now rests in plastic

with my father's, her Morse Code machine,
her Army uniform, moth-pocked in storage.
This is a dirge encrypted in things,
porcelain thimbles, seams sewn over

myths, facts resting with fiction,
exposed with their fine contradictions.

Three

The Trade of Escape

The film star drops out of the sky
when his prop plane loses an engine,
Tupac is shot, and his body-
guard, too. Both items are news
you hear as you wait on hold
on the phone in the office. The radio
broadcasts a mixture of sun & clouds
you can't see without windows.
The West Side Drive is backed up
for miles, a twenty-minute delay
expected, outbound
at the Williamsburg Bridge
and the Mid-Town Tunnel. Today
you rummage in your desk for an aspirin,
while the call you made makes you wait.
You draw small crafts in the margin
of a yellow pad, and forget who it is
you have called. Boats with outboard
engines, a float plane with its single propeller,
coast on a Pilot pen's ink, little black swells
form to a tune by Vivaldi that replaces
the news. A willow tree drops its weeping
leaves down one side of the page, and by now
you've left the building, the city.
The letters and phone have become
props in a stage for departure. How many
wings will it take to lift you, intact, over
the side of your cube by the mail room?
Every day deliveries come and go. Express,
Overnight, Second Day, Same Day. One day
a courier asks you which way is out,
and you follow the directions you gave him.

Portable Monitoring System

Nothing is safe from poetry.
Today, even the man in the yellow
hard hat, a Seismic & Acoustic
Monitor resting on subway cement
at his feet, makes the page. At first
I think it's a hoax. A mock episode
so close to Halloween. I imagine
the Richter scale of New York,
the seismic decibel of the F train
as I try to make a call. Today,
the rumble of wheels on steel
charms me, that we get there
faster than a cab, safer
than a bus, easier than either,
even walking, since it's raining.
Today, this dial lies open in a box,
with an arrow sitting still on its face
—not late, not early, not fixed on a thing.

The Pitch Forward

This is a type of extreme sport. A three-inch
"S" hook fits on the far limb of an elm tree,
my thighs pressed against the fire escape
so my hands stay free to hang a birdhouse,
your gift from the farm. I slip on the grate,
alone, catching myself and the bag of seed
before one of us drops three flights to the yard
below. I am dressed especially for climbing
out the window. I scrape my knuckles
the first time out. This is how I pitch
forward this morning. I leave
the rapids of my last great romance behind.
The past is the raft I let go. Some days
falling for you is a walk in the woods,
watching Great Blue Herons mate in the pines,
their stick legs drifting. Two osprey sail over us,
suspended in air. An old trick of theirs.
All the birds travel in pairs. Nothing risky
in that, I say to myself, putting the sooty screen
back in the frame, the window refusing to shut.

Geirangerfjord

A frayed rope strung through rods
served as a handrail to keep us
from slipping two-hundred meters down
into mist that rose from the falls.
Ingar held his hand out to assure me,
this was nothing. Audun watched
from the top. I clung to the cliff's wall,
the stone, ice cold, and stood on a sliver
of ledge under sharp white water
pounding in front of my face, dropping so fast
the camera could not freeze a frame.
My boots brand-new, my pack
made for books, I climbed an hour
to reach this place, breath stopped, eyes
caught, and only my intention to hold me.

November 7th

In the clotted lines on Election Day,
under basketball hoops
in the high-school gym,
I hope to see your face, overheated
like mine, our wool scarves wound
too tight. Crowded, but still it's too little,
too late for our candidate. I hope to
and hope not to see you
after a year. I did not change my address
on the books. The election is fixed
by everything done and not done
before this. My signature dates back to the year
we moved in, full of hope and hobbled
by fear that never left, undoing all the best
intentions, the campaign that failed
to outlive the election.

A Place to Live

Oh patron saint of apartments, oh benefactor
disguised as a landlord, thank you for the sink
in the kitchen, the light in the hall. Thank you
for the windows that open, doors that close,
for the bedroom, the closet, the rudiments
of home. Thank you for my place, this address,
the zip code, 10014, the mailbox and keys.
Thank you! Mr. Weinberg to the rescue!

Remind me of the doormen, the marble lobby
I gave up, the polished brass supporting the awnings.
Remind me of rooms with white moldings, six coats
of paint laid on smooth so it gleams, crystal finials,
porcelain lamps, Baccarat glasses, and flatware.
Goodbye, Rosenthal china! Remind me of dinners,
evenings spent without candles, so there's
no wax buildup on the ceilings, on the walls.

Remind me, Jonah Weinberg, a roof can be made
of the ribs, a home in the belly of a whale, remind me
of the ceilings. Oh perfect cracked ceilings on Carmine,
oh crumbling brick walls. Dance me through the history
of housing, of losing, of building new bookshelves,
the price of sunlight and soot that falls on this carpet
from Turkey that traveled with me from my past life and
lies here in the shadow of God, so far from Constantinople.

The bells from Our Lady of Pompeii on the corner
toll every hour. They toll for the steerage, the clutter,
the leaving of order, the sweating, the swearing, the forgetting.

Building a Nest

She fit the printed tissue pattern
flat over my chest, her fingers
lining the place where the seams go,
a circle over my shoulders, under my arms,
down my spine. The shapes she cut later
in fabric—seersucker for summer, boiled
wool in winter. This morning you press your hands
on the pale cotton sheets over my ankles
where the inseams go between my legs,
your lips pursed like my mother's, full of pins.

Coming & Going

You know how to write
directions. I see what's exposed
in the way you want to
get me there. Coming
and going. Each time I turn
the right way, just where you say,
"turn," where pumps
in the oilfields crank
but I don't hear their churning.
I listen to NPR on the air
and my windows are up
in the rental car. Coming,
I am so anxious. Every sign
has to be Los Feliz Boulevard
but isn't. I can't wait
to see you so much
I miss the road, clearly marked.
The one thing I didn't
write down, thinking I know
where you live by heart.

Nuclear Fruit

Never had Chinatown's market reeled
like a film on a set of salt fish and dried bone,
blue chard, red roe, roast ducklings strung
by their necks under heat lamps that blazed
in plate glass, unreal, like that night in
November we met. Not since the last time
I dropped acid, in college, not since then
have oranges and apples and figs looked so lit.
You are, one year later, still
the person I never imagined I'd pick,
the one I'd been hiding desire for, the one
perfect pear in the bin, overlooked,
nearly neon, richer and brighter than any other,
so late in the year.

Savings

I woke in a dream, a child pinching
white sheets off the line in winter,
the sun barely warm enough to dry them,
my hands, ice cold, grasping clothespins,
the sack to collect them frozen stiff
in my fingers. I dressed only to dash
from the porch through the snow
to the line strung between pear trees
and back. No hat, no gloves, my feet
bare in my boots to save time. We were
saving energy, saving money not using
the clothes drier in the basement.
The good bright sun did the work.
The wooden pins held the wash
in place in the draft, in the dream
of losing my mother, her lessons.

Subterraine

A dachshund in a pouch on the F train
stares blankly at a baby slung over
her mother's lap. We stand between them
rocking. You fit your hand in my
pocket. The infant has just noticed
the dog. Her eyes aroused, her lips
open as we enter a tunnel, leaving the sun
on the tracks of the bridge for this
deaf racket below.

Apostles: Black & White

They sit, gathered, in the bodega display case facing the street, next door to the sweaty auto-body shop I've been to twice today. A matched set. Two Last Suppers in stone, the width of a child's hand and half its height, are stuck between a pair of hermaphrodite candles and a red bleeding heart, the soul's stigmata, on the shelf. Both tableaux have Jesus leaning in, left of center, clutching robes to his chest, his apostles raptly doing the same.

One set is dark, as though a thumb had closed over their faces, leaving its smudged brown print. And the other, bleached white, seems startled, the flesh like the blanched underbelly of a fish, cooked. Of the two, the latter looks most out of place. It's a Mediterranean setting. I could almost rub the grease of olives between my fingers, imagine the sticky welt of wine on their tables as I stand, dizzy, in the heat. It's August, and I don't know how I'll pay for the car I wait for. I imagine a life with the constant buzz of a missing muffler, a daily dose of the toxic. I bite into a piece of fruit.

Jose and then Frank punch the clock, and later Eddie, who asks his boss for his pay, in advance. He hands me the keys. All three have places to rush to. A routine. I imagine the hotplates waiting for them. A home. A life. Or maybe not. Maybe tonight, just one of them will walk out of a well-laid lair, leave his wife, the mortgage, a soft bed, start an unsafe car and drive off to a feast he never planned on attending. When he walks in, amazed, he won't think where his next meal will come from. At that moment, the hardest choice he'll have to make is which table he's drawn to—which end of it—which seat.

Public Transportation

She is perfectly ordinary, a cashmere scarf
snugly wrapped around her neck. She is
a middle age that is crisp, appealing in New York.
She is a brain surgeon or a designer of blowdryers.
I know this because I am in her skin this morning
riding the bus, happy to be not young, happy to be
thrilled that it is cold and I have a warm hat on.
Everyone is someone other than you think
under her skin. The driver does not have
a peanut butter and jelly sandwich in his metal
lunchbox. He has caviar left over from New Year's
and a love note from his mistress, whom he just left
on the corner of Sixth Avenue and 14th Street.
When she steps off his bus to take over the wheel
of the crosstown No. 8, she knows she is anything
but ordinary. She climbs under the safety bar
and straps the belt on over her seat. She lets
the old lady who is rich but looks poor take her time
getting on. She lets the mugger who looks like
a parish priest help her. She waits as we sit, quiet
in our private, gorgeous lives.

Winter Climate

This morning Jill at the photo lab and Guadeloupe
at the newsstand join Phil, the super, and Greg,
who serves me, first, at the coffee shop. All of them
love me. They love me the way the policeman
who watches me pass Waverly Place every day
does, the way the girl in the blue muffler
on the bus does, her nose and mouth wrapped
so tight only her eyes give me the seat on the aisle.
They love me the way Ernesto, who hands me the mail,
checks my pulse without touch, the way the winter sun
burns my skin, for free, leaving a crease the way the wind
bites the parts of my face not covered. They love me
the way you would if you were here, the way I accept
what thrives on the street without knowing it, letting
this pass through me like love's winter climate.

Rethinking Regret

Let's thank our mistakes, let's bless them
for their humanity, their terribly weak chins.
We should offer them our gratitude and admiration
for giving us our clefts and scarring us with
embarrassment, the hot flash of confession.
Thank you, transgressions! for making us so right
in our imperfections. Less flawed, we might have
turned away, feeling too fit, our desires looking
for better directions. Without them, we might have
passed the place where one of us stood, watching
someone else walk away, and followed them,
while our perfect mistake walked straight towards us,
walked right into our cluttered, ordered lives
that could have been closed but were not,
that could have been asleep, but instead
stayed up, all night, forgetting the pill,
the good book, the necessary eight hours,
and lay there—in the middle of the bed—
keeping the heart awake—open and stunned,
stunning. How unhappy perfection must be
over there on the shelf without a crack, without
this critical break—this falling—this sudden, thrilling draft.

Notes

Dedications:

Coming & Going for John Kalish
Lunch Hour for Harold Steinblatt
Over My Head for Martin Mitchell
Rethinking Regret for Robin Becker
Sewing, A Sonnet for Denise Mitchell
The Prickly Bush for Michelle Valladares
Undressed in The Cloisters for Stephanie Craig
What Comes Back for Teddy Laurel

The title "The Flag of My Disposition" is based on a line from Walt Whitman's "Leaves of Grass."

photo by Lorinda Sullivan

Elaine Sexton's poems have appeared in *American Poetry Review,*
The Christian Science Monitor, New Letters, Prairie Schooner, and
numerous other journals. She holds an M.F.A from Sarah
Lawrence College, and is a graduate of the University of New
Hampshire. She grew up on the coast of New Hampshire, and
lives in New York City, where she works in magazine publishing.

New Issues Poetry & Prose

Editor, Herbert Scott

Vito Aiuto, *Self-Portrait as Jerry Quarry*
James Armstrong, *Monument In A Summer Hat*
Claire Bateman, *Clumsy*
Michael Burkard, *Pennsylvania Collection Agency*
Christopher Bursk, *Ovid at Fifteen*
Anthony Butts, *Fifth Season*
Anthony Butts, *Little Low Heaven*
Kevin Cantwell, *Something Black in the Green Part of Your Eye*
Gladys Cardiff, *A Bare Unpainted Table*
Kevin Clark, *In the Evening of No Warning*
Jim Daniels, *Night with Drive-By Shooting Stars*
Joseph Featherstone, *Brace's Cove*
Lisa Fishman, *The Deep Heart's Core Is a Suitcase*
Robert Grunst, *The Smallest Bird in North America*
Paul Guest, *The Resurrection of the Body and the Ruin of the World*
Robert Haight, *Emergences and Spinner Falls*
Mark Halperin, *Time as Distance*
Myronn Hardy, *Approaching the Center*
Edward Haworth Hoeppner, *Rain Through High Windows*
Cynthia Hogue, *Flux*
Janet Kauffman, *Rot* (fiction)
Josie Kearns, *New Numbers*
Maurice Kilwein Guevara, *Autobiography of So-and-so: Poems in Prose*
Ruth Ellen Kocher, *When the Moon Knows You're Wandering*
Steve Langan, *Freezing*
Lance Larsen, *Erasable Walls*
David Dodd Lee, *Downsides of Fish Culture*
Deanne Lundin, *The Ginseng Hunter's Notebook*
Joy Manesiotis, *They Sing to Her Bones*
Sarah Mangold, *Household Mechanics*
David Marlatt, *A Hog Slaughtering Woman*
Gretchen Mattox, *Goodnight Architecture*
Paula McLain, *Less of Her*

Sarah Messer, *Bandit Letters*
Malena Mörling, *Ocean Avenue*
Julie Moulds, *The Woman with a Cubed Head*
Gerald Murnane, *The Plains* (fiction)
Marsha de la O, *Black Hope*
C. Mikal Oness, *Water Becomes Bone*
Elizabeth Powell, *The Republic of Self*
Margaret Rabb, *Granite Dives*
Rebecca Reynolds, *Daughter of the Hangnail; The Bovine Two-Step*
Martha Rhodes, *Perfect Disappearance*
Beth Roberts, *Brief Moral History in Blue*
John Rybicki, *Traveling at High Speeds*
Mary Ann Samyn, *Inside the Yellow Dress*
Mark Scott, *Tactile Values*
Martha Serpas, *Côte Blanche*
Diane Seuss-Brakeman, *It Blows You Hollow*
Elaine Sexton, *Sleuth*
Marc Sheehan, *Greatest Hits*
Sarah Jane Smith, *No Thanks—and Other Stories* (fiction)
Phillip Sterling, *Mutual Shores*
Angela Sorby, *Distance Learning*
Russell Thorburn, *Approximate Desire*
Rodney Torreson, *A Breathable Light*
Robert VanderMolen, *Breath*
Martin Walls, *Small Human Detail in Care of National Trust*
Patricia Jabbeh Wesley, *Before the Palm Could Bloom: Poems of Africa*